FORAGING FAIRYTALES

Elderflower Festival

Foraging, Folklore and Food

Duncan Tinkler, Imogen Tinkler & Alicia Upton

ISBN: 9798515001094.

Dedication

To the Eldermother and all the Elderflower for all the memories you create.

P.S. Please don't pinch us in our sleep!

Contents

Introduction

The changing of seasons is a magical time. Sometimes it's sharp- the sudden drop into autumn can feel like falling off a cliff! You wake up and the sun has slipped away.

However, spring to summer seems a gentle transition, the last layers of winter shedding and the sun slowly blooming like a flower.

Many try to mark the start of summer, pinning it to a month, a day or a festival. I can be found eagerly checking my watch to mark the sunsets as the sun lingers longer and longer into the evening.

But as we all know, nature moves in mysterious ways, and she will not be rushed, coerced or predicted. She walks to the beat of her own drum.

Summer does leave signs, however, that she has arrived. In times gone by, country folk would watch for these clues, setting their watches to the waxing and waning of the moon. Any curious sun seeker need only look to the hedgerows for confirmation that the summer has indeed come again.

English summer begins with elderflower and ends with elderberries

English Summer is traditionally marked by the arrival of elderflowers- the explosion of bubbling white blooms across our hedgerows.

Well, the elderflower is finally here, and we think that this is cause for celebration. Come again is the season of sundresses, lazy outdoor evenings and lightly tanned, freckled (or perhaps a little burned) noses.

We're inviting you to join us in our seasonal celebration- The Elderflower Festival! Gather your friends, your family (and any four-legged companions) and head to the hedgerows. Fill your mind with the magic of elder folklore, your baskets with blossoms, your kitchen with flavour and your glasses with elderflower fizz- celebrate the return of a true icon of British summer time.

"English summer begins with elderflower and ends with elderberries."

elder flower

Fairytales

Fairytales and Folklore From The English Hedgerows

By Alicia Upton

Our wild spaces are steeped in folklore, with every hedgerow, woodland and open meadow humming with history and magic. The Elder has long been held as a queen of these wild and wonderful spaces, standing front and centre in the folklore of English Summertime.

Elders blossoms bring the summer- the frothy champagne fizz of a bottle popped in celebration of long, hot days. As her berries ripen and mellow, as do the seasons, the bright excitement of summer making way for the richly hued days of autumn.

Somewhat magnanimously, the Elder takes a similar role in folklore across the globe. In every nation where the elder sinks down it's roots, the same myth prevails- the myth of a shrewd and cunning tree spirit, which guards each and every elder shrub.

In Denmark, she is known as Hyldemor, a wise old dryad that dwells in the gnarled trunk of all Elder trees. The English know her as Elder Mother, or Lady Elhorn.

I picture the Elder spirit as a wisened and wise hedgerow witch. Eager to gift the blessings of her wisdom to those who request it, but quick to thwack your legs out from under you with her twisted walking stick should you test her good humor. Neither a friend or a foe, but a generous yet vengeful crone, to be respected and never, ever crossed. As we shall learn, hell hath no fury like an Elder Mother scorned.

A surefire way to bring down her wrath is to burn elder wood- a cardinal sin. Shropshire locals believed that burning Elder would call the devil himself to perch upon your chimney. It was avoided at all costs, for the fear it would bring his cloven hooves click-clacking across your roof tiles.

Lincolnshire country folk paint a similar picture of the elder- an old woman filled with vengeful scorn for those who cross her. Any parent foolish enough to lay their newborn in a crib of Elder could well pay the ultimate price. In the depths of night, Mother Elder would slip into the nursery and torment the child, pinching its tiny limbs till bruises bloomed black and blue. Worse, Mother Elder might kidnap the child and leave a wicked changeling in their place- a fae-child sent to torment the parents of the human baby.

As terrifying as these tales may be, it is important to remember that the Elder Mother is more than a wicked witch. She is also a wise and giving crone. She blesses our hedgerows not once, but twice a year, with a bounty to both feed and heal us.

Her berries and blooms are yours for the taking- providing you present an offering to placate her.

As a child I was always told to appease Mother Elder with a song. I still remember spending hazy summer days with my Ma, singing to Lady Elhorn as we gathered buckets of blooms to make cordial. However, more sinister tales tell a different story, suggesting any eager forager must pay a higher price. These stories suggest those hoping to harvest from the Elder need offer a limb or two:

"Lady Ellhorn give me of thy wood,
And I will give thee of mine,
When I become a tree."

Old English Folklore

Signing away your body (even after your passing) seems a tall price to pay for a bough of Elder. I much prefer to sing whilst I harvest- anyone based in Cornwall best keep an eye (or ear) out for me as I hum and sing my way around the hedgerows.

Lady Elhorn also acts as guardian of the dead, a pagan equivalent to the greek legends of Charon. The Elder Mother is known to be a gateway guardian- protecting not only her own flowers and fruits, but the veil between this world and the next.

This reputation has earned it a home in many a graveyard, ast is said to protect the spirits of the recently departed as they travel to the afterlife. Believers in its power would often lay their loved ones to rest beneath the boughs of an Elder, in the hope it would bridge the barrier between heaven and earth. Not only would it protect their loved one, but convey a message from the afterlife. A thriving elder above a grave is said to mean the deceased is safe and content on the other side.

As is the way of the Elder, this gift of protection and comfort is double edged. As we know, the Elder has its branches in the land of the living, but sinks down its roots to the other side. Those stopping beneath elder to rest awhile on a midsummer's eve may find the veil uncomfortably thin. Folklore has it that Lady Elder isn't the only spirit eager foragers and hedgerow wanderers need be wary of.

The sweet, intoxicating perfume of elderflower is familiar to any seasoned forager. It's known to hypnotize passers by, leaving them drowsy and intoxicated with it's heady, sweet aroma. Those lured into the elder's honey trap may find themselves victim to the maleficent whims of fae-folk, who have been known to emerge from their mystical realm and whisk wanderers away to their faerie feast, never to be seen again.

So, as you head out to fill your baskets this summer (singing, of course, as you go), consider the hidden duality of this much loved (and often feared) tree. Keep your wits about you and remember: never burn or build with the branches of an Elder, or you might just fall victim to the vengeance of Mother Elder. gift a song or two as you harvest the abundance of this season's crop.

Myths and Legends From The Emrald Isle

By Imogen Tinkler

"He saw fuchsia in a drizzling noon
The Elderflower at Dusk like a risen moon
And green fields greying on the windswept heights."

Extract from Glanmore Sonnets by Irish poet Seamus Heaney.

I grew up listening to folklore passed down to me by my Mother and Great Uncle Harry. None were more magical than the Elderflower, so let me take you on a journey through Irish myth and legend.

In Ireland it was considered a sacred tree and just like the hawthorn it was forbidden to be cut down. I love the fact that it grows in the most desolate of places from cracks in our urban cities, to crumbling buildings abandoned throughout the countryside to finding gaps in the hedgerow and taking hold. This amazing tree has been celebrated for generations for its culinary, medical and magical uses.

An old Irish saying states there are three signs of a cursed or abandoned place "the elder, the nettle and the corncrake". An abbot in Iona created a law that women and children were not allowed to be killed in warfare and anyone who broke this law would face ruin and future generations cursed. They would come back as elder, nettles or corncrake Which is why if you look closely at the bark you can see its creases, rough like the skin of a person who has lived many lives. The Elder was universally held to be an unlucky malevolent tree and in Ireland was considered to be mischievous as most fairies are. It was seen as foolish to make a cradle out of edler as the children would sicken and the fairies would steal them.

It was also believed "He who sleeps under an elder will never wake" so I was always worried to nap under it as a child. It does have some loose basis in science - the living bark, leaves, roots, blossoms and berries possess a strong aromatic and oil based chemical, often referred to as a narcotic, whis is powerful enough to deter exploring rabbits and livestock. In fact much of the Elder tree is toxic. At Samhain the last of the elderberries were picked under magical rites. The wine made from these berries was considered the last sacred gift of the Earth Goddess. It was drunk ritually to invoke prophecy, divination and hallucination.

The Elder is considered to have a 'crostail' or bad temper of mischief and it was believed that someone who was struck with an Elder Branch - that after their death their hand would grow out of their grave. I would often look in the graveyards to see if there were any hands appearing as a small child having heard this story many times.

It was also said that it was wrong to strike an animal or child with a piece of Eder as it would stop them growing from that day onwards. My Great Uncle Harry was struck by a drunk school teacher at school by an Elder branch. He burst Harry's drum and Harry suffered with deafness from then on. He was also a small man and I used to believe he hadn't grown because of this. I thought this was very unfair. Surely it should have been the drunk school master that should have been punished. I always believed there was something very fairy-like about Uncle Harry and that he could have been friends with Moonface, Saucepan Man in Enid Blyton's classic The Faraway Tree.

There are some good uses for the Elder Tree too. I was always taught that a wreath made from Elder leaves wrapped around a milk churn could protect milk from bad spirits and keep it for longer. Elder was traditionally planted around dairies to stop milk from "turning" and cheese clothes and other linen involved in the dairy process were hung out to dry on eldertrees. The smell they absorbed from the leaves may have contributed to hygiene in the diary.

Elder trees were also traditionally planted by baker's houses as protection from the Devil. Inside the baker's houses there are hot ovens where the devil loved to live inside. So loaves and cakes were put out to cool under the Elders and rid them of any bad spirits. Any food left out overnight under the Elder was considered a gift to the fairies.

The Elder tree is sometimes called the "hollow tree! Because the spongy tissue within its smaller branches can easily be removed thus providing hollow tubes. I was always taught these hollow insides led into the fairy Kingdom. I spent many a night with my Mama creating stories of adventure through the Eldertree. My favourite being that the Eldertree had the power to walk in twilight and peer into a childs window making sure a child was safe and asleep. I really believed that our Elder Tree looked over me while Mama was at work at night. I always felt safe that the fairies would look after me as Mama, uncle Harry and I respected the tree.

While many revere the Elder due to the fairy folk. It was considered lucky to have one growing near your house. Traditionally a Ronaw would be grown at the front and an Elder Tree at the back door. To keep evil influences from entering your home. I am always delighted that we have one in our neighbours garden that spills over into ours.

The sweet aroma from the elders leaves has long been known to repel flies so this folklore may have been borne out of the need to keep insects and diseases that they carried away from the kitchen and food.

Bunches of leaves were hung by doorways, in livestock barns and attached to horse harnesses for the same reason. To keep the flies away.

Legend also suggested that if a young girl washes her face in the morning dew of the elderflower she will remain young. Extracts of elder are used in skin cleansers today so maybe there is some truth in it! The berries from the elder also were used to dye grey hair and keep one youthful.

If you wanted to see witches you were told to anoint your eyes with the green juice from the elders inner bark.

The Elderflower is even seen in scripture . In Ireland it was believed that the Elder Tree refused to shelter Christ but the Ivy did. From Then on the Elder is the last tree co come into leaf while the Ivy is Evergreen.

It really is the most magical of trees. Why don't you make up your own fairytales of folklore with your own family and create stories to pass from generation to generation?

Elder Mythologies From The Native Americans

By Duncan Tinkler

When I think of Native Americans I am guilty of being influenced more by old cowboy films than real life. In my mind I see feather headdresses, redskins and peace pipes. I also hear the very haunting, smooth montage music as my 'Indian Brave' is at one with nature and sending smoke signals across the vastness of the landscape. I'm relieved to learn that the music, at least, is authentic.

As Elder is so easily hollowed out, the Native Americans would fashion branches of the tree into their famous Elderberry flutes and pan pipes. These beautiful instruments would produce the ducet yet haunting melodies that we so keenly associate with the American First Nations.

To me the music they produced conjures feelings of awe and wonder, of the vastness of the lands these Nomadic people once roamed. But the question I should be asking myself is, does it make me sleepy, or actually keep me awake?

According to one Miwok Legend, a guy called How Tol-le-loo wanted to steal some fire from a village. His plan was simple, he took with him an Elderberry Flute which he started playing as he entered the village, and soon enough everyone around him was falling asleep.

When the last person finally dropped off, Tol-le-loo crept over to the dying embers of the fire, and was just about to take them when a robin called Wit-ta-bah swooped down and covered the embers with his wings.

This doesn't stop our man Tol-le-loo though. He whips out his flute and starts playing with it once again. Soon enough Wit-ta-bah is sound asleep, still covering the embers with his now reddened chest.

Rather than simply lifting up the little bird, Tol-le-loo decides to cut a hole in the poor little chap's wings and steal the fire that way. As Elder doesn't burn very well, Tol-le-loo uses his flute to store the embers as he makes his escape from the village and up the mountains.

From another Miwok legend, the Birth of Wik'-Wek and the Creation of Man, we get this passage describing a single Elder tree, the Lah-pah, in the world at the dawn of time, located 'where the sun goes up' in the east and guarded by 'a den of rattlesnakes':

"Its branches, as they swayed in the wind, made a sweet musical sound. The tree sang; it sang all the time, day and night, and the song was good to hear. Wik'-wek looked and listened and wished he could have the tree. Nearby he saw two Hol-luk'-ki or Star-people, and as he looked he perceived that they were the Hul-luk mi-yum'-ko—the great and beautiful women-chiefs of the Star-people. One was the Morning Star, the other Pleiades Os-so-so'-li. They were watching and working close by the elderberry tree. Wek'-wek liked the music and asked the Star-women about it. They told him that the tree whistled songs that kept them awake all day and all night so they could work all the time and never grow sleepy. They had the rattlesnakes to keep the birds from carrying off the elderberries."

Eventually, Wik'-wek secured some of the Elder tree which he planted across the country, offering the American Indian people food, music and medicine.

These wonderful stories go a long way to show just how important the Elder tree was to these people. As the medicinal value of the plant is dubious at best (interestingly used as a remedy for cold and flu on both sides of the pond, despite there being little scientific evidence that it works), and the flowers and berries being a great supplement to the diet, but never a main course, to the Native Americans the true magic of elder lay in it's music.

elder flower

Foraging

The Kitchen Table Guide to Foraging

We were called hunter gatherers for a reason. We hunted and we gathered. The hunting part was quite tricky, it involved pointy sticks and wild animals. When we started farming and invented a bow and arrow it became less of a necessity and more of a sport. The gathering part on the other hand remained an integral part of everyday life for most people right up until the industrial revolution.

Unfortunately after that it became less and less important so much so that it is now an almost forgotten skill. But what exactly is foraging? How can it be good for us, our families and even the environment? And how can we know that we are foraging safely, legally and ethically? What are the potential risks? Well, follow this guide and you can't go far wrong.

What exactly is foraging?

According to the Cambridge Dictionary Foraging is a verb meaning 'to go from place to place searching for things that you can eat or use'. Which is fair enough, but then scrumping could quite easily fall into that category, and I certainly am not condoning any of that milachy.

To me, foraging is much more than that. It's getting outside, alone or with friends and family, going for a walk and coming home with delicious and nutritious things to liven up your food life. It's appreciating the wonder of nature, becoming in tune with the seasons and building real connections not only with the outside world, but with those around you. Foraging is therapy, it's mindfulness, it's exercise and it's healthy. Done thoughtfully and with care it can also be great for habitat and biodiversity.

Another thing that foraging can be is overwhelming and scary. There are millions of plants out there, most of which are inedible, either because they are just disgusting, or in some cases poisonous. In the Kitchen Table Revolution we remove overwhelm and fear by teaching one thing to forage a week.

How is it good for me and my family?

Our hunter gatherer ancestors evolved eating what they could find, when they could find it. For this reason many foraged foods contain exactly the right nutrients for the time of year. For example nuts and berries that are high in energy are prolific in the autumn, a time that we would have needed to pile on the pounds in order to survive the winter.

This is also true of wild garlic which comes out in the spring. It is a great source of vitamin C, which would help fight off scurvy as well as enhance collagen, which helps protect the skin from sun damage.

Also, farmed foods tend to be selected for size and flavour, with little care given to their nutritional content. In contrast, wild foods tend to have a much higher nutritional value. For example 'fat hen' has more iron than spinach and vitamin B than cabbage.

Not only is wild food better for us, the act of foraging- getting out into nature, getting exercise and spending quality time with our families is great not only for our physical health, but our mental wellbeing too.

How can it be good for the environment?

By swapping even a small part of our food each week with something grown in the wild, we are relying less on mass produced 'factory' farming, reducing food miles and encouraging biodiversity.

Industrialised farming tends to use chemical fertilisers, pesticides and herbicides to produce crops in the quantities demanded by supermarkets. These 'agrochemicals' are produced in factories, transferred to specialist storage facilities and then distributed to farms, where they are sprayed on the crop.

Each stage of this comes with it's own (sometimes significant) risk to the environment. Whilst these risks can be avoided by 'going organic', this is often an expensive option and can be cost prohibitive. Foraging, on the other hand, is free.

Moreover, food grown for supermarkets (no matter how organically it is produced) will often be distributed far and wide from its place of origin. Whilst being able to eat exotic fruits from far flung counties is amazing, and something we, in this modern, globalised world should be rejoicing, it comes with a price.

In order to remain fresh, food is often wrapped in single use plastic and travels day and night in power hungry climate controlled vehicles. By supplementing some of your food with something wild you can significantly reduce the food miles, and in fact have a positive impact on the environment.

By foraging mindfully (taking just what you need, a little from each plant and leaving enough for the birds and the bees) you are actually playing into nature's hands. Plants that are edible, are edible because they want to be eaten. Either it's a way to pollinate, or disperse seeds. Or a way to be pruned to encourage new growth, either of it's self or by allowing light through to sapings below.

A habitat that is regularly foraged tends to have higher biodiversity. As more and more edibles grow they attract hungry herbivores and in turn predators. As the habitat becomes more popular with foragers and other nature lovers it is much more likely to become respected and protected.

Elderflower- fresh, local and great for pollinators!

How do we forage safely, legally and ethically?

Foraging mindfully means taking what you need, a little from each plant and leaving enough for the birds and the bees. This approach does need the application of a little common sense, but if done right, it should mean that what you are doing is sustainable.

As a beginner to foraging it is sometimes difficult to gauge the amount of a given plant you will be needing, and bringing a set of scales with you is often impractical. In the Kitchen Table Revolution I usually avoid weights and measurements in favour of terms like 'a good handful'. I tend to use ratios too, as if you can visualize how much of the end product you want, knowing how much of the raw ingredient to forage should be relatively straight forward.

It is illegal to take the root of any plant in the wild in the UK as this is not only harmful for the individual plant, but the habitat in general. Instead, pick leaves, flowers and berries with care. Taking all the leaves from one plant will almost certainly kill it- leave enough so it can breathe. If you're taking flowers, be aware that they almost certainly will become some kind of fruit if left alone. You might want to come back later in the year, or leave some for the birds.

Be aware of how many other plants of the same variety are in the area, or how scarce that plant is in general. If you are amongst a sea of wild garlic you can be a little more ruthless than perhaps if you're seeing only one or two rare violets every few feet.

It never hurts to take a guard dog along (although Olive here is rather bashful!)

It's not advised to stray from public footpaths, especially if that involves trespassing on private land. But if you do find yourself doing a 'Red Riding Hood', then be careful not to trample down the undergrowth or destroy ground nests and the like.

Farmers famously like to chase people off their land brandishing shotguns with dogs at heel. Avoid this by asking permission first. More often than not they will be as happy as Larry to let you forage from hedgerow and field borders- as long as you're not scrumping their apples or worrying their livestock. In fact, farmers tend to know quite a bit about wild edibles, so you might find yourself with a mine of information.

Lastly and perhaps most importantly, be absolutely certain you know what you are picking. If you are anything less than 100% sure what it is, it is best to leave it alone. By bringing a field guide with you (preferably one that doesn't require batteries,

for example the book you are currently reading) you should be able to have a good idea of what you are looking for.
If in doubt, take clear photos of the plant, it's leaves (and if possible flowers) as well as noting the habitat you found it in, and run it past an expert. Luckily, The Kitchen Table Revolution has experts coming out of it's ears. A good few of them know a thing or two about foraging too.

Personally I would avoid foraging mushrooms until you have a little experience, and apart from fennel (as the smell is such a give away), avoid the carrot family. You don't want to serve up Hemlock soup to your inlaws. Well you might, but you will get in trouble if you do.

In general it is quite tempting to try and learn everything at once. This can lead to overwhelm and ultimately death. To avoid this we teach one thing a week, and gradually build up our knowledge throughout the year.

Potential risks when foraging

Picking for edible wild plants, when done with a little common sense and knowledge, is a relatively safe thing to do. However, there are some risks that should be taken into consideration before your first foray into foraging. First and foremost, it is worth repeating that you should make sure that you are 100% sure you know exactly what it is that you are foraging, and that it isn't poisonous. If in doubt, leave it alone.

Once you have picked something edible and taken it home, the risk doesn't necessarily end there. I'm sure that everyone on a blackberry hunt has 'accidentally' eaten more than ended up in the basket, and almost nobody has ever gotten ill from it. But blackberries tend to be high up, away from potential dog wee and poo that could cause illness. Personally I would avoid low hanging 'fruit' next to footpaths where dogs are frequently walked. If it's unavoidable, wash your bounty thoroughly, especially if eating raw.

Toxoplasma gondii is a parasite that is very occasionally present on the surface of plants and more likely in cat poo. If you are foraging in an area where cats like to shit (more likely a problem for the urban forager), then make sure you thoroughly wash everything, and preferably cook it. Even if you do catch toxoplasmosis you should be ok (unless you're pregnant or have a weakened immune system) as it only causes flu like symptoms.

Botulism is a rare disease that is caused by the bacteria Clostridium botulinum, a bug that can grow in food that is stored and preserved with low levels of oxygen, i.e. pickling, oiling or infusing. As preserving and foraging often go hand in hand, it is something that should be given due consideration.

For any bacteria to grow it will need a combination of food, water and air. Most preserving techniques deprive the bacteria of at least one of these, creating an environment that is unsuitable for their growth. For example, both sugar and salt 'occupy' all the available water when dissolved in it to a certain concentration and won't allow bacteria to grow. Unfortunately Clostridium Botulinum is a sneaky bugger. It will find free water within the plant matter, and needs little oxygen to grow.

By drying foraged goods before using them you are reducing the amount of available water, and therefore the risk of the bacteria growing. However this may have detrimental effects on the flavour and texture of the finished product.

If you are using them fresh in infusions (such as vinegars, oils and sugar syrups) thoroughly sieve out the plant matter using a muslin, pillow case or clean cotton sock (honestly, makes a great sieve). By drastically reducing both food and water for the bacteria you are almost entirely eliminating it's preferred environment. To be on the safe side, it is advisable to heat the product to 75°C or 167°F for at least 30 seconds

Finally, when doing any preserving make sure that all tools and containers are sterile at the point of use. The simplest way to do this without affecting the outcome of the product is with heat, either placing in a pan of boiling water, running through a dishwasher (on a high heat), or popping in an oven at above 100°C or 212°F for 5 minutes. Keep the items in the sterile environment until the last possible moment and use sterilised tongs to handle them. By combining all of these things you should be safe in the knowledge that you have done every possible to significantly reduce any risk of illness.

Should you ever feel unwell after eating anything foraged, always seek medical advice immediately.

Grab a basket and get out there!

Elderflower Foraging

May - July

The hedgerows are bubbling with Elderflower and a haze of it's sweet, ethereal scent is perfuming the countryside. They are the perfect thing to forage- whether you have never collected natures bounty before or you're a seasoned pro.

Let these pages guide you -telling you what to look for, where to find them and what darstardly doppelgangers you might find on your adventures!

The Elder

The Elder can vary in size- from a small shrub to a huge tree.

Buds

Before they burst into flower, buds are a bright lime or buttercup yellow colour.

Blooms

Elderflowers bloom in bursts of creamy white flowers. Each little flower has 5 petals, each of which is framed by shooting pollen tipped stamens.

Leaves

The leaves of the Elderflower are serrated, and commonly group in clusters of 5.

Perfume

One of the most distinctive things about elderflowers is the smell: floral, creamy and 'Summery'. Quite often you can smell the scent as you get closer towards the plants. Elderflowers should not smell like wee, musty or damp. If they do, find fresher smelling blooms.

When should I pick it?

The best time to pick it is on a hot June afternoon when the blooms are fully open. If you aren't covered in pollen after you harvest they aren't open enough. Don't pick it after the rain as all the pollen is washed away.

Where will I find it?

Elder is a hedgerow shrub that grows just about everywhere. Many people have trees in their garden, and it can often be found on roadsides and footpaths.

How much can I pick?

If you are foraging from a huge tree, don't worry about leaving enough for the birds and the bees, they can fly up to the blooms you can't reach. Do worry about leaving enough for other foragers and for the elderberries that appear towards the end of summer.

What can I do with it?

As soon as you get home, infuse Elderflower in sugar water to make cordial or syrup. You can use it to make delicious wine or fizz, and it goes really well with crab and pork.

Use these photos as a reference when you head out to the hedgerows, fields and footpaths to forage!

Dubious Doppelgangers

In discerning dopplegangers, your nose is your best friend.

Elderflower has a distinctive, citrusy and summery smell to it, that should easily distinguish it from anything else. Luckily, the closest thing in appearance to Elder is Rowan, the flowers of which are edible, and can be used in much the same way- nothing to worry about there.

Rowan flowers look similar, but just don't smell nice- a dead givaway!

What is potentially more worrying is the resemblance to Hemlock, a notoriously poisonous plant famously used in the execution of Socrates in ancient Athens. One to try and avoid if you can.

Whilst the plant itself is vastly different from the Elder tree, the flowers can look similar, and there is potential for accidental picking if done so in a rush. Take your time, and make sure that what you are picking comes from a tree or a bush rather than a single green stem from the ground.

Toxic doppleganger Hemlock grows from the ground on a single stem.

Hemlock has small, angular star like flowers. Flies love them- we don't!

My Top Elderflower Foraging Spots

A foragers biggest asset isn't a beautifully rustic wicker basket, or even the hardiest of walking boots. It's the knowledge of their local area- what grows where, and when. It's this knowledge that keeps their basket full each season, and their larders well stocked.

In the Kitchen Table Revolution, we walk through the seasons one forage at a time, working weekly to expand our knowledge, pack our cupboards and delight our bellies. As the years go by, we learn to anticipate the wild flavours of the seasons and gathering iconically seasonal forage (like elderflower), becomes an important and valued tradition.

As June creeps closer I find myself excitedly returning to the same spots week on week, eagerly watching for the emergence of Elder's frothy white blooms. Like many a forager before me, I just can't wait to fill my boots.

It's a seasonal traditional that awakens childhood nostalgia. I can vividly remember spending sunny afternoons picking elderflowers with my family, the baking sun releasing the heady, sweet perfume. Year on year, we'd return to the same hedgerows and footpaths to harvest nature's bounty.

I encourage you to use these pages almost like a diary. Jot down where you find your elderflower blossoms, so you can return year on year, building seasonal rituals that will become treasured memories. Come autumn, you can even return to harvest the elderberries (providing you've left some of the blooms to mature) and join us in celebrating the hedgerow festival.

elder flower

Recipes

A delicious twist on our elderflower oil recipe.

Our Favourite Flavour Combinations

The true taste of summer, elderflower has a delicate, citrusy, grassy flavour that is so much more than a cordial or sparkling wine. It's natural sweetness automatically lends itself to summer fruits such as strawberry, raspberry and cherry, and can be countered by the sharpness of lemon. This goes exceptionally well with mint, for example in our elderflower and mint fritters.

Infusing the floral aroma into a nice white wine vinegar makes for a wonderful, summery salad dressing and can be used to make a great mint sauce that goes so well with new season lamb or goat (we're not kidding!). Why not try making our Asian Elderflower Marinated Pork Belly? It's perfect for a summer BBQ. Even those who swear blind they don't like elderflower will be begging you for the recipe!

Elderflower is also delicious paired with seafood, particularly things like smoked salmon, trout, crab or lobster. We have served up this simple crab and elderflower bisque at our famous supper clubs a few times now, and get such a great reaction every time!

Top tip: you really don't want to rinse elderflower under the tap as you'll wash away all the nectar and pollen. Instead, just leave out for a while and all the creepy crawlies will scurry off!

Our Simple Kit List

I know when I see a kit list as long as my arm - it makes me feel overwhelmed and want to shut the book straight away. So here is our simple guide to what you need!

A muslin- but if you don't have one a pillowcase or a clean cotton sock works just as well. The perfect use for those pesky odd socks and they do make a great sieve!

Jars - ask friends and family to save jars for you to put your lovely treats in. You could even fill one to give back as a gift.

Bottles - ask friends and family to save bottles for you. We use plastic two litre bottles for our Elderflower Champagne as it can be very gassy and exploded glass ones isn't good for us or the environment. Plastic is a godsend when we don't use it for single use. Glass can actually be the worst packaging option because of the high energy demand in bottle production and its weight in the transport phase. Even if you reuse a glass bottle 8 times it isn't as energy efficient as a plastic bottle that is used once. However the issue is how they are recycled as plastic bottles can potentially end up in the sea.

Fermenting Bucket or a 10 litre container - you can pick these up at boots fairs, Facebook MarketPlace and by just asking friends and family if they have one they don't use. Or you can purchase them at your local brewing shop, Wilkos or the Range. You can of course order online and it will come whizzing to your door. They are normally £10 and under and we use ours for so much - from Nettle Beer to salt making to Elderflower Wine. It is one of our most used things in the kitchen!

Funnel - you can buy one locally if you don't have one or you can use an old plastic bottle and create your own.

Pots and pans - just the everyday ones you have in your kitchen.

Elderflower Cordial

Makes: 2 Litres Time: 30 minutes + overnight infusion

We use more Elderflower in our recipes then most - this makes the coridal stronger and more concentrated so you get more from each bottle. Like fairy liquid! i

You will need

40 ripe Elderflower heads

2 litres of boiling water

1 kg of caster sugar

2 tsp of citric acid or half a cup of lemon juice

Method

1. Check the flowers for any insects, place them in a bowl and pour over the boiling water.

2. Cover loosely and leave to steep overnight.

3. Strain Elderflowers through a muslin cloth (if you don't have a muslin cloth a pillow case works well) into a saucepan.

4. Add the sugar and citric acid (orlemon juice) and bring to the boil.

5. Reduce the heat and simmer for a couple of minutes.

6. Leave to cool and pour into a sterilised bottle or jar and put it in the fridge.

Top Tip: To make Elderflower Syrup, use half the amount of water

Add a little magic to your glass by freezing edible petals into your ice cubes! We've used forget-me-nots and dasies.

Elderflower Iced Tea

Makes: 2 Drinks Time: 5 minutes

There is nothing like a long refreshing drink on a hot summer's day. Especially after you have been out foraging Elderflower and creating Cordial! So make this quick and simple recipe to enjoy the fruits of your labour.

Make this recipe your own while getting creative in the kitchen. Try different flavour combinations with different teas! We tried this with an English Garden Tea from a local independent brand we love - Chai Wallah Margate. It has apple and mint notes and it is so good! We may have added some gin too as a Sundowner. Pure Bliss.

You will need

125ml of boiling water

15 large ice cubes

40 ml Elderflower cordial

1 Earl Grey tea bag
(or tea of your choice)

Half a lemon

A good glug of gin (optional)

Method

1. Pop the teabag in a large teapot or bowl and pour over the boiling water.

2. Leave to infuse for 90 seconds.

3. Mix the ice, cordial and lemon juice in a jug.

4. Pour the hot tea into the jug and mix until it is cold.

5. Pop ice into tall glasses or teacups along with a glug of gin (if you're having) and pour the tea over it. Enjoy!

Top Tip: Always brew your tea in a warmed pot.

Elderflower Oil

Makes: 500 ml Time: 45 minutes

This is the perfect way to preserve your Elderflowers to use them throughout the year. We have used a Grapeseed Oil as it has a high smoke point and because it's virtually flavorless, it lets the Elderflower really shine!

It will last for a month in the fridge or you can freeze it to keep all year for the winter months. We love to freeze it and give it to our friends and family in their Christmas Hampers. They absolutely love it!

You will need

20 ripe Elderflower heads

500ml Grapeseed oil

Method

1. Check the flowers for any insects and cut off the stalks.

2. Pop the oil and elderflower in a saucepan on a low heat until the elderflowers wilt.

3. Remove the pain from the heat and leave to infuse until cold.

4. **Strain the oil thoroughly** through a muslin cloth (if you don't have a muslin cloth a pillow case works well).

5. Pour into a sterlised bottle or jar and put it in the fridge.

Elderflower Vinegar

Makes: 500ml Time: 45 minutes + 2 weeks infusion

This is another great way to preserve your Elderflower so you can use it throughout the year. We use a Chardonnay Vinegar, but any White Wine Vinegar will work.

The fresh, zingy and floral flavour of Elderflower Vinegar can transform all sorts of dishes. Use it to add some magic to pickled vegetables, or a beautiful note to a salad dressing. I have even added it to a Gin and Tonic to give a tart flavour- delicious!

You will need

20 ripe Elderflower heads

500ml Chardonnay vinegar

Method

1. Check the flowers for any insects and cut off the stalks.
2. Stuff them into a large jar.
3. Pour over the vinegar.
4. Pop the jar in a pan of water (the water should cover the jar) and bring to the boil.
5. Once it has been brought to the boil turn off the heat and leave to cool in the water.
6. For best results leave to infuse for two weeks in the fridge and then **strain well through a muslin cloth** (or pillow case). You can then store it for up to a year.

Top Tip: You can always transfer to a glass bottle to gift or serve. It looks so much prettier!

Elderflower Bubbles

Makes: 8 Litres Time: 1 hour + 10 days fermantation

Elderflower bubbles are as quintessential to British summer time as strawberries and cream (incidentally, they're a wonderful combo). It's one of our favourites- a deliciously floral and devilishly intoxicating drink that is almost as easy to make as it is to consume!

We learnt the hard way that it's best to make this in plastic containers. The fermentation process generates a buildup of carbon dioxide, which is powerful enough to burst through even the sturdiest glass bottle. What a mess!

You will need

1kg sugar

15 heads of Elderflower

4 lemons - juice them and peel them to use the zest in strips

2 litres of boiling water

6 litres of cold water

½ tsp yeast nutrient

Optional: 5g sachet Champagne yeast

Muslin Cloth (or a clean pillowcase)

10 litre container (a fermenting bucket is perfect but don't be put off if you don't have one - they're widely available to buy and at under £10, still cheaper than a bottle of champagne!)

Funnel

4 2 Litre plastic bottles

Method

1. Check the flowers for any insects and trim off the stems.

2. Dissolve the sugar in 2 litres boiling water in your container or fermenting bucket. Leave to cool.

3. Add the cold water, lemon peel, the juice of 4 lemons, yeast nutrient and the elderflowers and give it a stir to allow the air in.

4. Add a pinch of champagne yeast now if you have it - it is ok if you don't as Elderflower has wild yeasts so it can be interesting to see what happens. We reccomend you have some in a few days' time, to add in if nothing happens.

5. Cover with a muslin cloth and leave to ferment at room temperature for 5 -6 days, giving it a little stir everyday. You will notice it starting to fizz and bubble as the process begins! If after 3 days nothing is happening add in some champagne yeast.

6. We use plastic bottles for the next stage as the plastic bottles have a little more give than a glass bottle.

7. Pour the elderflower bubbles through your sterilized muslin cloth (or pillowcase) using your funnel. Tightly screw on the lids and store in a cool place - we put them in our shed.

8. Leave the bottles for 3-4 days checking them each day and carefully open each lid to let some of the gas escape if needed. If you put them in the fridge it will stop the fermentation completely.

9. Now you can enjoy them - they can last for ages - we have even had one a few years later that was left hidden in the back of our shed - what a treat to find!

Imogen's favourite!

Xanthê's favourite!

Elderflower Gummy Bears

Makes: 20 Bears Time: 15 minutes + setting time

Our little girl Xanthê absolutely loves these! If you haven't had a chance to make your cordial yet I think this will spur you on. If you have - hurrah! Have a dance around your kitchen to celebrate.

Today you will be making your very own gummy bears - or whatever shape you fancy! Get creative - you can add edible flowers to them and even alcohol for a very adult treat.

You will need

1/2 a cup of Elderflower cordial

1/2 teaspoon of agar agar (or you can use gelatin instead)

Moulds to pour it into- if you don't have moulds you can use ice cubes trays and even add some edible flowers. They look so pretty like this!

Method

1. Pour the Elderflower Cordial and agar agar into a pan.

2. Heat on a low heat and stir until the agar has dissolved and the mixture has the consistency of a syrup (7 - 10 mins). If adding alcohol, add whilst it cools.

3. Pour Mixture into molds.

4. Pop in the Freezer until set.

5. Enjoy!

Elderflower Turkish Delight

Makes: 50 Pieces Time: 2 Hours

Turkish Delight is a magical treat. Whenever I sink my teeth into the soft, pillowy sweetness I feel instantly transported to a magical world- through the wardrobe to a land of talking lions and evil Ice Queens. Well, forget wicked White Witches- this turkish delight is flavoured by the queen of summer: Elderflower.

It's an easy way to enjoy the flavor of summer all year round, and makes a beautiful gift. Best of all, it's so easy to adapt! Why not try using a different floral syrup to flavour?

Top tip: This is definitely a recipe for two pairs of hands! That was a lesson I learnt the hard way.

You will need

400g sugar

300ml of water

2 tsp lemon juice

75g Cornstarch

Elderflower Syrup to taste (see elderflower cordial recipe)

Extra Cornstarch/Icing sugar to dust (depending on how sweet you like it!)

Method

1. This recipe is a sticky one! So to start, grease an oven dish with a flavourless oil (I used vegetable) and line with baking paper.

2. Grab a large, heavy bottomed pan and mix together your first three ingredients: your sugar, lemon juice and 180ml of your water.

3. Bring this mix up to boil over a medium-low heat, and keep it rolling until your sugar thermometer reaches 120 Celcius or 250 Fahrenheit. You don't need to stir one the sugar's dissolved, but be sure to scrape down any crystals that form on the sides.

4. Whilst this mixture heats, combine your cornstarch, cream of tartar and remaining water in a separate pan. Be sure to whisk thoroughly and continuously to avoid lumps! These would form hard lumps in your sweets, so should be avoided at all costs.

5. Place this mix over a medium heat and bring to a boil, whisking constantly. The mixture will gradually thicken. Now would be a good time to bring in your second pair of hands!

6. Once the syrup has reached 120C, remove it from the heat. Gradually combine it with your cornstarch mix- adding a little at a time and- you guessed it- whisking continuously.

7. Once fully incorporated, reduce the heat to low and leave to simmer. You (and your helper) can rest your well whisked arms, as at this point it only needs whisking every 6- 10 minutes to avoid the sugar caramelizing on the bottom of the pan.

8. Leave over the heat for up to an hour, stirring every 6-10 minutes to ensure the bottom does not burn. Your mixture will become golden and transparent, and will reduce in volume.

9. What you're waiting to judge here is consistency. To test this, dip a little on the end of the spoon into a glass of ice water. Once cooled, give the mix a taste test- has it reached the chewy yet soft consistency of your favourite turkish delight? If so, it's time to add your Elderflower! If not, leave to simmer a little longer.

10. It's Elderflower Time! Stir in your syrup to taste- using the same ice-water technique to judge the flavour. Keep an eye on the texture too- adding liquids may make your sweet a little too soft. If so, keep over a low simmer for a short while longer.

11. When you're happy with your mix, pour it into your lined baking tray. Use a spatula to even it out.

12. Once cooled, dust a clean surface with your cornstarch/ icing sugar. Turn out the cooled turkish delights and slice into cubes. Ensure all sides are well dusted and enjoy!

Top tip: Be careful when working with hot sugar, as it can cause serious burns.

These are just divine! Perfect with coffee for an afternoon treat.

Elderflower Custard Creams

Makes: 4 large biscuits Time: 45 minutes

Do you love custard creams as much as we do? Well now you can make your own at home.

They're almost too good to be true! The first batch I made were so good we ate them all before we took a picture - oops.

These delicious treats are really easy to adapt- why not add your own twist? Get creative with tea and rustle up some Earl Grey Custard Creams. I went all out last year and made Gorse Flower and Lilac. They looked so beautiful, I didn't want anyone to eat them!

You will need

For the custard biscuit:

170g Butter (keep it out of the fridge)

55g of icing sugar

170g of Self-raising flour

55g Custard powder

For the cream:

50g of Butter

100g of Icing sugar

1 Teaspoon Elderflower Syrup

Method

1. Preheat your oven up to 180C.

2. Grease 2 baking trays with a knob of butter.

3. Mix the butter and icing together in a large bowl until light and fluffy.

4. Slowly add in the flour and custard powder bit by bit until the mixture forms a paste.

These are almost too good to be true!

5. Divide into little balls and pop them on your baking tray.

6. Use the back of a spoon to flatten each ball - light touch (unless you are trying to do this with a toddler).

7. You can create your own designs on them with a fork.

8. Bake for 12 ish mins - you want them to be golden brown and dry on top.

9. Leave them to cool - ideally on a rack.

10. Now to make the buttercream filling! Mix the butter, icing sugar and Elderflower syrup. Feel free to adjust the syrup measurements to taste.

11. Spread your elderflower butter cream onto half your biscuits and then pop the the other halves on top.

Elderflower Tart

Makes: 1 large tart Time: 1 hour + chilling time

If you were to ask me what my ideal summer day might look like, my answer would be simple. A sunny countryside wander to a secret cove, a scrumptious picnic topped off with a slice of this heavenly tart and a glass of chilled elderflower fizz.

It's slick parisian patisserie meets the ethereal sweetness of the english hedgerows. A match made in heaven! Best of all, it's so versatile- top it with your choice of fruits and edible flowers. It's the perfect opportunity to get out foraging, or head to a local pick your own. Why not try to find some wild strawberries?

You will need

For the pastry:
300g Flour

200g Butter (cold, diced)

100g Sugar

A Pinch of Salt

A little cold water (Optional)

Fruits and flowers of your choice to top

For the elderflower custard:
300 ml whole milk

4 egg yolks

50 g caster sugar

50 ml elderflower cordial undiluted

35 g cornflour

100 ml double cream

Method

1. Add your Flour, sugar and salt to a bowl and combine. Next, add your cold, diced butter to the bowl and rub between your fingertips to create a crum like texture.

2. Knead the dough gently to bring it together. If it seems too dry, now is the time to splash in a little cold water.

3. Add your Flour, sugar and salt to a bowl and combine. Next, add your cold, diced butter to the bowl and rub between your fingertips to create a crum like texture.

4. Knead the dough gently to bring it together. If it seems too dry, now is the time to splash in a little cold water.

5. Continue until a smooth dough forms. It is important not to overwork the dough- use a gentle touch and don't knead for too long.

6. Place your dough in a lightly floured airtight container and leave to cool in the fridge for 30 mins- 1 hour.

7. Whilst the pastry is chilling, it's time to get started on your elderflower custard! First place your egg yolks, sugar and elderflower cordial in a bowl and whisk for a few minutes, until combined.

8. Sift in your cornflour and whisk until smooth.

9. Slowly add the heated milk into your egg mixture, whisking as you pour.

10. Pour this mixture through a sieve, back into the saucepan and place on a low heat, whisking constantly (arecpie and a workout!). Bring the mixture up to a boil for a couple of minutes.

11. Pour the now thickened mixture into the saucepan into a bowl. To prevent a skin forming, place parchment paper on the top of the custard. Cover with a plate and pop it in the fridge alongside your pastry to cool

12. Preheat your oven to 180 degrees C.

13. Roll out your dough on a lightly floured surface to an even 1cm thickness. Use this to line your pastry tin.

14. Line your pastry case with parchment paper and fill with baking beans. You can get small ceramic balls from any shop with a baking selection, I however have a tub of dried mung beans that do the job!

15. Bake in your preheated oven for 15 minutes. Remove the beans and paper, and bake for another 5 before bringing out to cool.

16. Back to the elderflower custard! Remove from the fridge and whisk. It will seem stiff at first, but keep on- it will gradually become smooth.

17. Whip your double cream to a soft peak and stir into the custard. You should have a smooth, delightfully creamy elderflower custard.

18. Spoon this into your cooled pastry case and smooth to an even thickness.

19. Now for my favourite part! Grab your berries, fruit and edible flowers and use them to decorate the top. I love to use strawberries for a traditional summer flavour, but invite you to go crazy!

20. Serve with a glass of chilled elderflower fizz.

We topped ours with sttrawberry and mint, for a fresh, summery flavour.

Elderflower and Mint Fritters

Makes: 10 Fritters Time: 20 minutes

The first time I made these deliciously crispy little bites of pure summer was live on Facebook for our weekly Sunday Brunch Club. Luckily they are so quick and easy that my lack of preparation wasn't a problem! They came out perfectly first time and before we knew it we were demolishing them all day long.

They are perfect as a garnish on both sweet and savoury dishes, or as a snack on their own. If you have a sweet tooth, simply sprinkle a little icing sugar over the top before serving.

You will need

1 large organic egg

50g / 1/3cup Self Raising Flour

250 ml / 1 cup milk

A good handful of finely chopped mint

Zest of 1/2 small lemon finely chopped
A pinch of salt

10 elderflower heads.

About two inches of cooking oil

Method

1. Preheat the oil in a deep sided frying pan until smoking hot

2. Beat together the egg, flower, milk, mint and lemon zest to make a thin batter (add more or less milk as needed, it should be the consistency of pancake batter, which is what it is really)

3. Dip in the elderflower heads, holding them by the stalk.

4. Carefully place them in the hot oil and watch them sizzle.

5. After about a minute they should have changed colour to golden brown, texture like sun.

6. Take them out and allow to cool on kitchen towel

Seriously Scrumptious!

Asian Elderflower Marinated Pork Belly

Serves: 6 adults Time: 3 hours

Summer is without a doubt my favorite time of year. Long, lazy, hazy days drinking beer and Barbequing fantastic foods feeding friends and family is when I am at my happiest. This simple marinade is perfect with pork, but goes oh so well with chicken or aubergine.

I always cook chicken and pork (including sausages) slowly in the oven before finishing off over the searingly hot coals. This way not only can I replace the worry of undercooked salmonella with delicious chargrilled yumminess, but I save time at the grill too.

You will need

600g / 1.3lb Outdoor reared Pork Belly (works just as well with chicken or mixed veg).

4 tbsp Wild Garlic Hot Sauce (or you can use ketchup, chilli and crushed garlic)

4 tbsp Elderflower vinegar

3 tbsp Soy Sauce

3 tbsp Local Honey

Thumb sized knob of fresh root ginger finely chopped (don't bother peeling it)

Salt and Pepper
More chilli (if you can handle it!)

Method

1. Preheat oven to 160° (140° fan or 284° or 320° fan, or gas mark 3).

2. Score the belly pork through the skin with a sharp knife (cut about half an inch into the flesh).

3. Mix all the ingredients together and using your fingers, massage thoroughly into the meat.

4. Put meat in a baking tray and cover in tinfoil.

5. Shove into the oven for 2 hours.

6. Remove from the oven and save all juices.

7. Finish off on a hot BBQ, using juices to baste as you cook. Turn regularly.

8. After about 20 minutes, slice into thick slabs, cover in the rest of the juices and serve.

My mouth's watering already!

Crab and Elderflower Bisque

Serves: 4 adults Time: 1.5 hours

There are two secrets to a really good bisque. The first is an excellent fish stock. These can be bought from fishmongers and posh supermarkets, but it is so simple to make your own and is much cheaper.

When you pick up your crab as if they have cat scraps, heads, bones and cut offs - these will often sell for pennies if not give away for free. Shove these in a saucepan with a halved onion (skin on, for colour),celery, carrots, a bit of fresh fennel (can be foraged quite easily), salt and pepper, and cover in boiling water. Allow this to simmer gently while you're doing the rest of the prep. It'll be ready when you need it.

The second secret is to use the shell. By smashing it up small and heating it you are able to release loads of flavour and that distinctive colour. If excavating the meat yourself seems like a lot of effort, simply buy dressed crab and ask for some extra shells. If this isn't possible a pint of shell on prawns will do the trick nicely.

You will need

A good glug of olive oil

A massive knob of butter

2 or 3 shallots, diced

1 carrot. Diced

1 Stick of celery, diced

1 clove of garlic, crushed

½ tube of tomato puree

I decent sized Crab (approx 200g of white and dark meat) including the shell

11 / 2pints fish stock

Good glug of brandy

4 tbsp Elderflower Syrup

2 bay leaves

Zest and juice of one lemon

A good glug of double cream

Method

1. Remove all the meat from the crab, and set to the side. This can be fiddly!
2. In a tea towel, with a rolling pin, bash up the shell until it's in tiny pieces.
3. Put Shell in a large saucepan with the lid on until it's smoking hot.
4. Cover shell with fish stock replacing the lid reducing heat to low.
5. In a separate frying pan heat oil and melt butter on low heat.
6. Add shallots, carrot, celery, garlic and bay to frying pan.
7. Keeping heat low, stir up veg before putting a lid on.
8. When soft (3 mins or so) add tomato puree, lemon juice, zest and brandy and stir.
9. Cook for a further 5 minutes before removing bay leaves.
10. Allow onion mix to cool before whizzing up.
11. Meanwhile carefully sieve shell out of fish stock.
12. Mix dark and white crab meat with whizzed up onions.
13. Mix this with fish stock.
14. Add Elderflower syrup before serving.

elder flower

About Us

The Kitchen Table Revolution

Time is the one thing you can't bottle and keep forever.
Our children are only little for a while
Those moments we want to keep forever
Yet we feel guilty when we are all in the same house doing different things.
We want to be the parent that plays all day but sometimes there are things to do.

In lockdown we all got to spend more time together as a family.
We were able to make banana bread and cook from scratch
But sometimes we just wanted a meal out
To not have to look in the cupboards and think what are we making again.

We went for walks but they could get boring. We are all human!

That is where the Kitchen Table Revolution came in for us!
It gave us a sense of purpose.
Some days we didn't feel like going on a walk
We lost our youngest daughter Beatrix the day before lockdown started.
We just wanted to turn over and hide from the world.
The world really did stop when she died
But we had a three year and we couldn't.

So we launched the Kitchen Table Revolution to give us a sense of purpose and to help with overwhelm.
We found it didn't just help us but so many others.
Take Cathy for example living with three generations under one roof - it gave them a sense of purpose to get out there and find Wild Garlic on their walks making it an adventure rather than just another walk.

One of our members said before she joined that she "thought it was for hippies with too much time on their hands" now she couldn't imagine another way it is protected time for her and her family.

We are human too - Alicia loves Parma Violets - I am not the biggest fan but we found lots of revolutionaries loved them. On a Saturday morning in torrential rain, Duncan, Xanthêand I set off into the woods to find violets. A few expletives left my mouth, Xanthê wailed and wanted to stay in the car. Then we got out into the woods with our waterproofs on and everything changed.

We felt calmer and happier, that feeling of day to day overwhelm went. Then we found the violets! There was much shrieking and I felt euphoric. If you had told me ten years ago I would have felt euphoric from a walk in the woods I would have told you that you were mad. Coming home and making them live in the Kitchen Table Revolution felt amazing. We were so proud. Then three weeks later we had to make a PINK cake for Grandpa for his birthday.

Xanthê was so proud as she decorated her special cake for him with her sugared violets. She told him it was a cake made with the happiest of memories so it would make you happy when you ate it. I was not particular happy getting up at 7am to make it before Xanthê went to nursery but the evening before had gone in a blur and there was no time. However it was so worth it seeing Grandpa's face and her pure delight as she gave it to him.

Join the Kitchen Table Revolution today at:
https://bangersandballs.co/kitchen-table-revolution/

So what is the Kitchen Table Revolution?

It is a community of families who come together to learn how to preserve and make one thing a week. It really is that simple. We know overwhelm is what stops us learning so we want to make it as easy as possible.

We preserve one thing a week from Edible Flower Rub, to my personal favourite booze from Elderflower Wine to Sloe Gin to Duncans infamous hot sauces from Rhubarb Hot Sauce to Cranberry Hot Sauce. We have experts inside to really help you from our off grid expert Jack who can help you with what you are growing to Vicky Felman who runs Canterbury Baking School. She taught us how to make a sourdough starter and sour dough bread - our first attempt failed as Xanthê decided to feed it roast potatoes - not quite how it works. We have the fabulous Arther Kane who led Stir it up Sunday which is traditionally when you all come together to make your Christmas pudding. It was so fun to all come together from each other's kitchen tables as we made a Christmas pudding together ready for Christmas. It felt so special when we tucked into it together at Christmas.

As that is what life is really about the memories you make with family, the time you spend together and the bonds you create.

In lockdown we all had too much time together and we were desperate to get out. Now as invitations come back, activities start to fill up our schedule there is a real fear that the time we valued will disappear.

So join us in the Kitchen Table Revolution and protect some time each week to do things as a family. Build those bonds that last a lifetime. Create reasons for your future little ones to come home from Stir it Up Sunday to Marmalade making day in January. This is really makes us family.

Join the Kitchen Table Revolution today at:
https://bangersandballs.co/kitchen-table-revolution/

Join Now

It doesn't matter if you live in the middle of London or out in the country- there is so much to find everywhere. One of our favourite places is Burgess Park near the Old Kent Road in London. It's amazing how much there is! Or now we are based in Whitstable where we have sea and countryside at our fingertips.

Now is the perfect time to join as we enter the Time of Plenty - there is so much bounty out there and it is a great thing to do over the summer! To help get you started we will send our brand new Elderflower Festival Book to you with amazing recipes from Elderflower and Crab, to Elderflower Syrup to my personal favourite Elderflower Champagne. Join for three months for only £45 and we will also send you our Hedgerow book in September. The best thing about this is you are joining a community of like minded people. Who all want to connect and do more in nature.

They know it makes you feel better, that it releases sertion and it helps you connect as a family. Even though we know it is good for us we all lack the motivation sometimes to do it. This community will inspire you and get you going. If you don't enjoy it - guess what you can unsubscribe -there is no 30 days notice period or anything like that. We aren't the gym and we want families to join who absolutely love it. Whether you are a grandparent or a mother or father this is a brilliant way to do things together. It gets the thumbs up from our three year old.

Being in tune with the seasons and what is happening outside has really changed my life for the better. I feel happier, I have more energy - Duncan and I have lost weight as we are more mindful of what we eat and have more energy. People are always telling us they love the way we parent. We feel a bit embarrassed but there is something magical about heading off on adventures and finding all sorts of things. Though not when she treads in dog poo - or tried to smear it on her face once. She hasn't done that again.

It makes us enjoy our time together more and not feel guilty when we all sit down in front of the TV. It has also made us more environmentally friendly as we think about where our food comes from. Xanthê asking where her corn on the cob at nursery came from is a personal favourite or where paint comes from in B&Q and does it have a season?

Taking our kids out there and getting them curious about nature makes them more inquisitive about everything and can only help their development and learning. So come and join us today. Do something to create time and memories for your families. The years are short and this is something that will bond you for a lifetime.

See you on the inside. We can't wait to welcome you.

Join now for £22 per month - less than the price of a large slice of cake and tea every week!

Join the Kitchen Table Revolution today at: https://bangersandballs.co/kitchen-table-revolution/

Duncan Tinkler

Duncan Tinkler has always had a keen interest in food- from growing up playing on the mud flats in Leigh on Sea, Essex eating the best cockles, to spending lots of time with family in Suffolk. This is where he fell in love with local and seasonal produce, learning to experiment and create amazing flavour combinations from his family's kitchen table.

Duncan has a keen eye for science, and storytelling and brought this all together with his wife Imogen when they created Bangers and Balls - Starting a Revolution from your Kitchen Table. He lives in Whitstable, Kent (where Scuba Diving was invented!) and spends many hours on the beach with his daughter Xanthe and rescue dog Spartacus. He can be found cooking outside in the most beautiful of places.

Imogen Tinkler

Imogen Tinkler has been fascinated with fairy stories and the magic of the natural world since she was a child, when she would create special worlds outside in nature with her Mother that allowed children to be children and adults to escape. After a successful career in the third sector working to change behaviours and create social mobility, Imogen decided to create Bangers and Balls - starting a Revolution from your Kitchen Table with her husband Duncan.

She lives in Whitstable, Kent, famous for its oysters and pirate alleys with their daughter Xanthe and rescue dog Spartacus. She can often be found bobbing about in the sea as a keen wild swimmer.

Alicia Upton

Alicia Upton has always been connected to nature. From a young age she spent her summers in the great outdoors, playing barefoot with the chickens in the garden and gathering fresh elderflowers with her family. These experiences have blossomed into a love of the natural world; she now finds joy through foraging, hiking and the occasional sea swim. This inspired Alicia to read Sustainable Product Design at Falmouth University in Cornwall.

Alicia inspires people to get outside, benefit from being out in nature and to cook delicious, nutritious food. She lives in Falmouth, Cornwall, with the sea a stone's throw from her window. She can be found (rain or shine) meandering across the wild Cornish landscapes.

Next in the Series

Follow us at on Facebook, Instagram and Twitter, so you never miss out on the next in our series! Why not sign up to our mailing list (at www.bangersandballs.co) to get weekly emails filled with delicious seasonal recipes, exciting seasonal tips and a few surprises. You won't know how you lived without it!

September 2021 will see the launch of our Foraging Fairytales Hedgerow Guide and in October we'll be bringing you our Foraging Fairytales collection. We are brimming over with exciting stories and recipes to share with you!

We love to hear from you too so do send us an email (at info@ bangersandballs.co) if you have loved this book or even just want to say hi. It is our community that makes us what we are.

From the Bangers and Balls - starting a Revolution from your Kitchen Table.

Duncan, Imogen and Alicia

Printed in Great Britain
by Amazon

62420569R20058